CANADIAN CONTEMPORARY
REPERTOIRE ES

FUN SELECTIONS OF JAZZ - POP -

LEVEL TWO

CONSERVATORY CANADA™

For more information about Conservatory Canada
and its programs visit our website at:
www.conservatorycanada.ca

Office of the Registrar
Conservatory Canada
45 King Street, Suite 61
London, Ontario, Canada
N6A 1B8

© 2009 Conservatory Canada
Published and Distributed by Novus Via Music Group Inc.
All Rights Reserved.

ISBN 978-1-49500-537-4

Novus Via Music Group Inc.
189 Douglas Street, Stratford, Ontario, Canada N5A 5P8
(519) 273-7520 www.NVmusicgroup.com

Preface

Canadian Contemporary Repertoire Series: Fun Selections of Jazz, Pop, Latin and Folk Music Level Two offers grade two students twenty-six appealing pieces at varied levels within the grade requirement. Students will develop technical and musical skills with user friendly repertoire from entrance level to preparatory grade three works.

Repertoire selections have been based on grade appropriate keys, time signatures, accompaniment figures, degrees of difficulty and length. Jazz styles include preparatory rags like *Beach Party Rag*, which leads comfortably to *Cotton Candy Rag* complete with stride bass, syncopated melodies and octave displacement. Boogies include works like *School's Out Boogie* and *Bill Grogan's Goat*. *Blues for You* and *Indigo Blues* provide varied accompaniments and blues scale playing. Students will be delighted by the swing rhythm of works like *A Night on the Town,* and *The Day Columbus Landed Here*. The lovely jazz ballad, *End of Holiday*, jazz prelude *The Forest at Twilight* and jazz waltz *The Cuckoo is a Funny Bird* are just some of the jazz titles offered in this collection.

Students will be rockin' to titles like, *Can't Stop the Rock* and *Dorian Disco*, while Latin dance rhythms are included in works like, *Tuesday Tango* and *Fado*. Arrangements of folk songs, *Land of the Silver Birch* and *The Kelligrews Soiree*, provide a strong sense of Canada's musical heritage, while the jazzed up version of *Old MacDonald* is just plain fun.

Conservatory Canada wants to keep music students studying longer! We understand the benefits gained through the study of music and we believe that students will remain engaged and excited about their studies if that music is current and familiar.

This is why we developed the Contemporary Idioms curriculum. Students can now be assessed and accredited through a program that involves contemporary styles of music such as Swing, Blues, Latin and Rock.

Conservatory Canada supports Canadian composers. This book contains pieces that are either original compositions or arrangements by Canadian musicians. All the selections in this book are eligible for a Conservatory Canada Contemporary Idioms examination. The pieces have been chosen with attention to proper pedagogy, skill development and student appeal. We hope you enjoy them!

TABLE OF CONTENTS

A Night on the Town

Tyler Seidenberg

With soul (swing the 8ths)

Blues for You

Fishel Pustilnik

Beach Party Rag

Debra Wanless

Rag style, not too fast

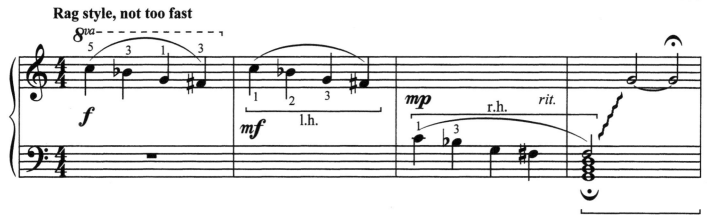

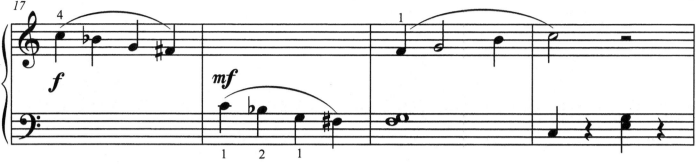

Beach Party Rag 2 / 2

Boogie

on Bill Grogan's Goat

arr. Andrew Harbridge

Fast (swing the 8ths)

Can't Stop the Rock

Tyler Seidenberg

Driving

Cotton Candy Rag

Janet Gieck

Allegretto with straight 8ths

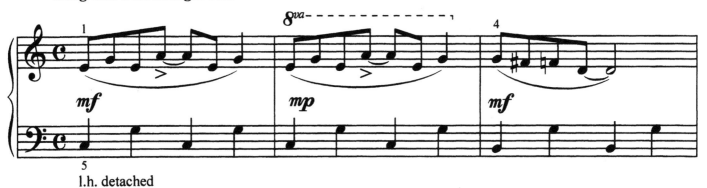

l.h. detached

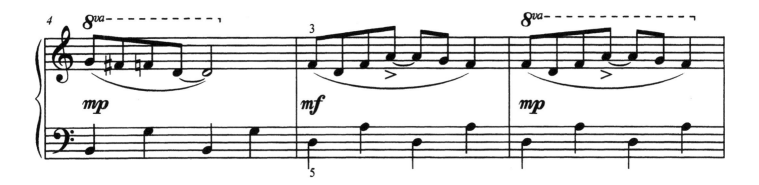

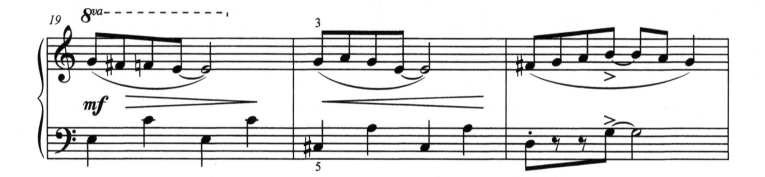

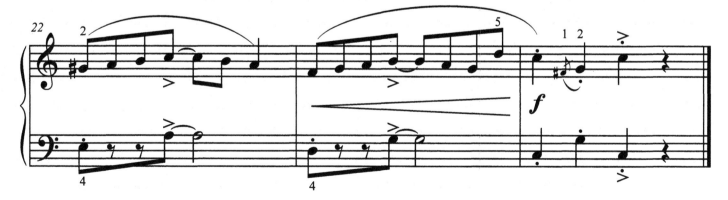

Cotton Candy Rag 2 / 2

Dorian Disco

Andrew Harbridge

With a steady beat

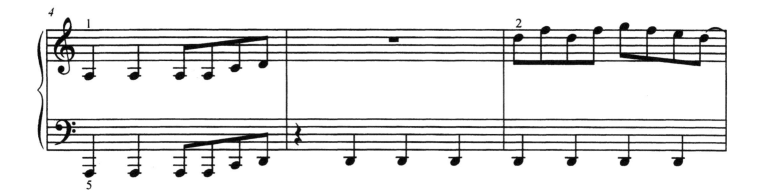

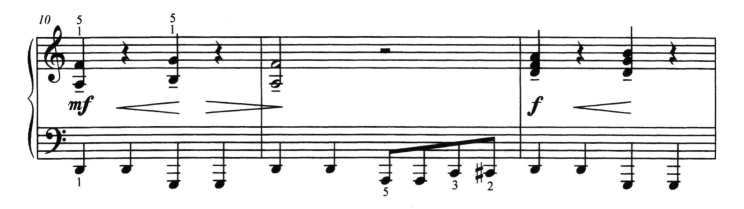

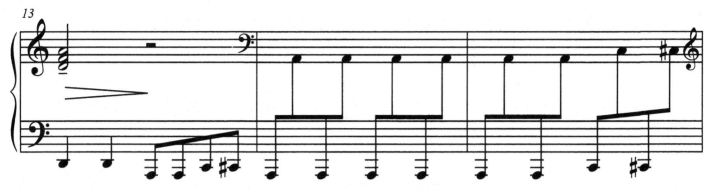

Dorian Disco 2 / 2

End of Holiday

Fishel Pustilnik

In a Blue Mood

Robert Benedict

* Improvise your own right hand melody for the repeat. Use the notes from the extended A Aeolian mode written below.

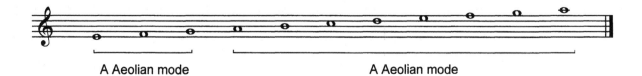

A Aeolian mode   A Aeolian mode

Fado

David Story

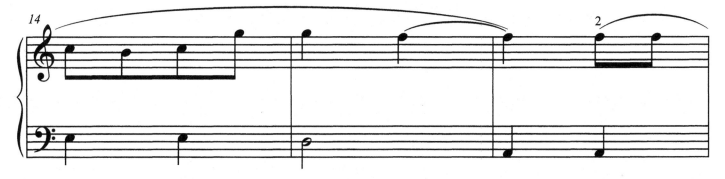

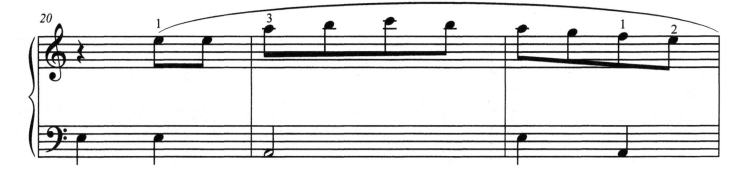

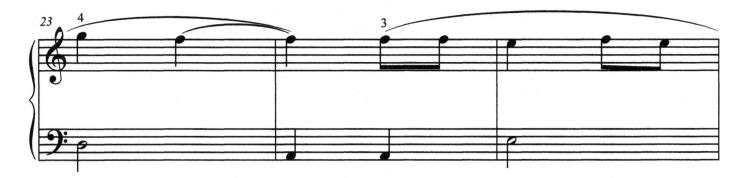

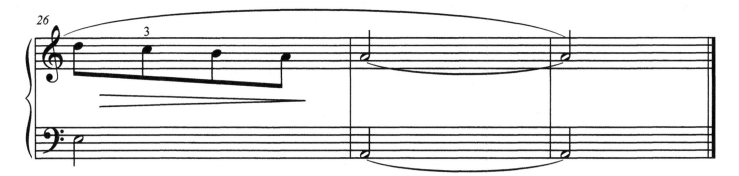

Fado 2 / 2

Indigo Blues

Joyce Pinckney

Swing rhythm

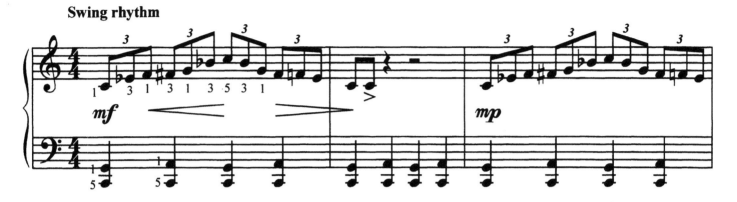

Land of the Silver Birch

arr. John Sandy

Loner

Fishel Pustilnik

Slowly, with expression

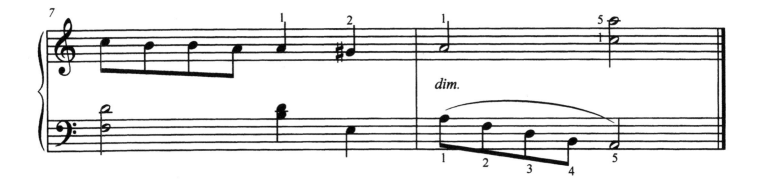

School's Out Boogie

Debra Wanless

Snappily

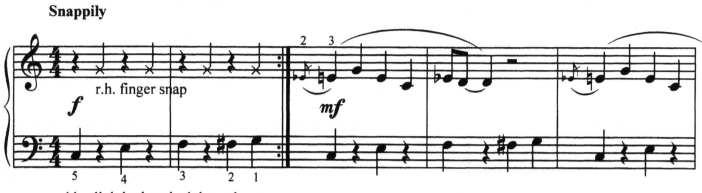

r.h. finger snap

l.h. slightly detached throughout

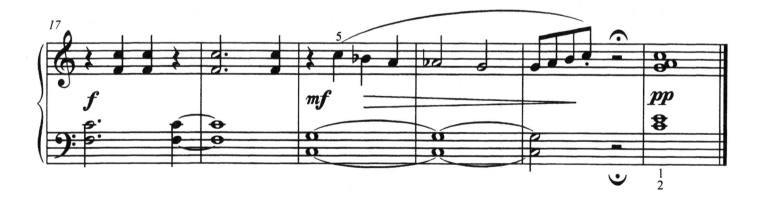

Old MacDonald's Swingin' Farm

Tradition
arr. Brian Usher

With Energy (swing the 8ths)

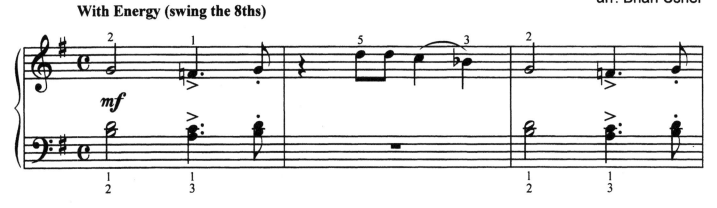

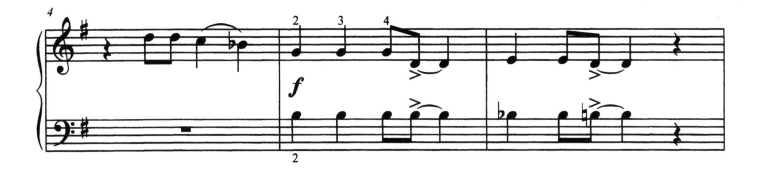

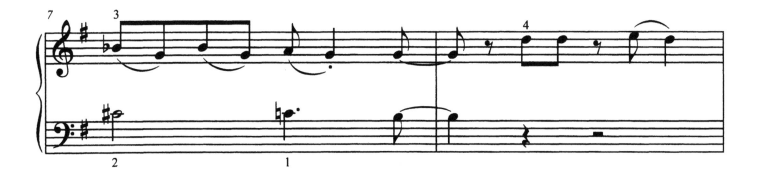

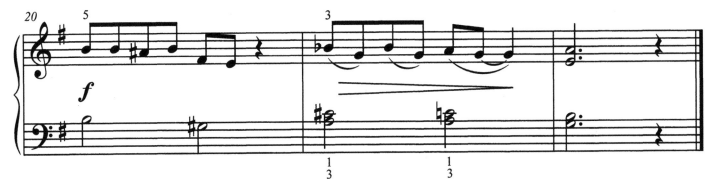

Old MacDonald's Swingin' Farm 2 / 2

On the Wings of the Dawn

Andrew Harbridge

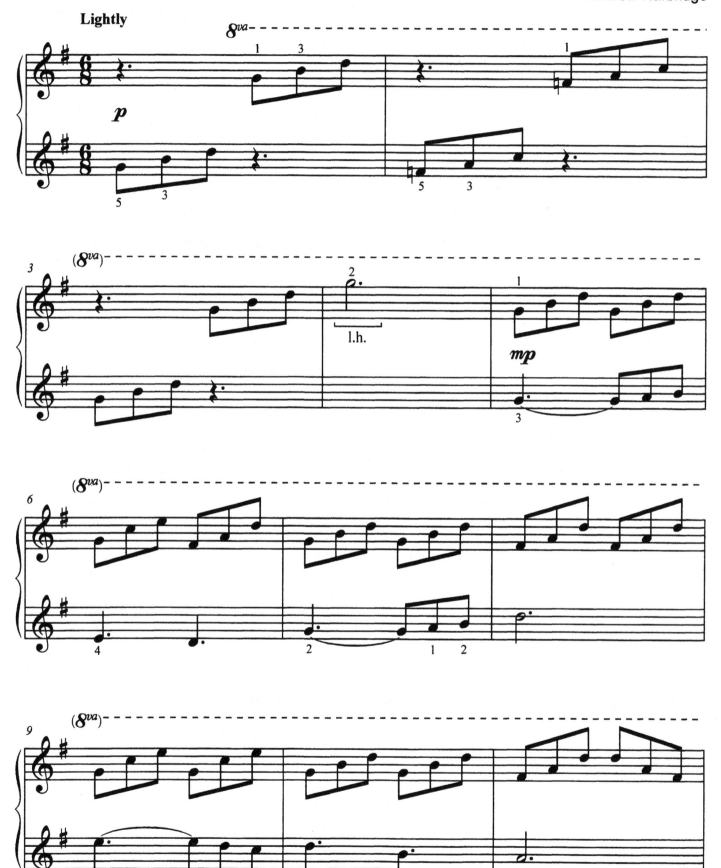

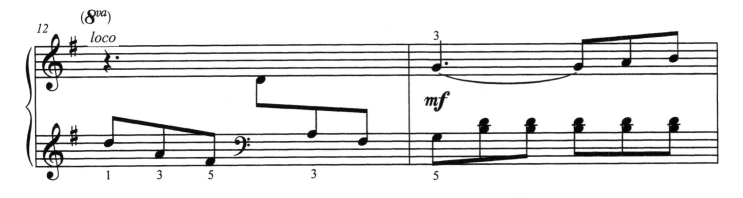

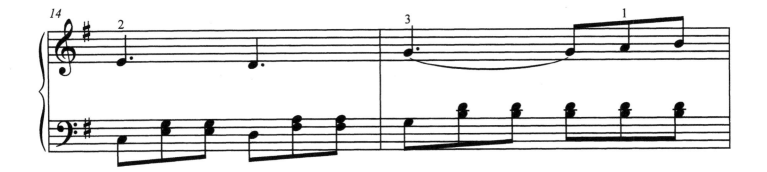

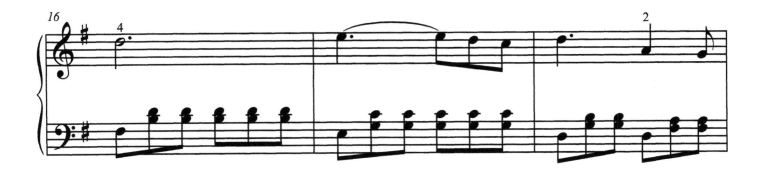

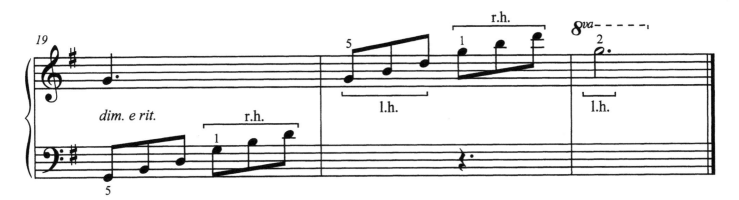

On the Wings of the Dawn 2 / 2

Sea Shanty

arr. John Sandy

Not too fast

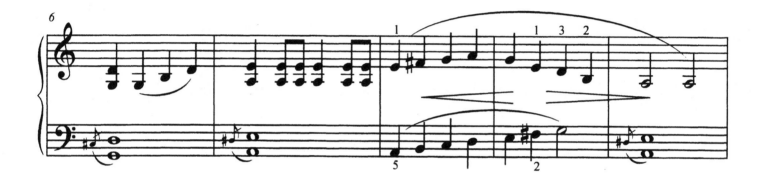

The Day Columbus Landed Here

Canadian Folk Song
arr. Fowke/Johnston

Not too fast (swing the 8ths)

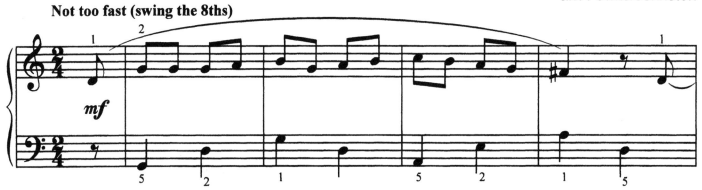

l.h. slightly detached throughout

Soft Pedal Blues

Sheila Tyrrell

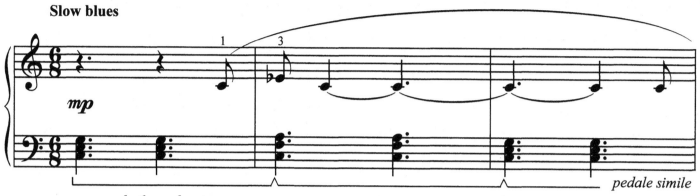

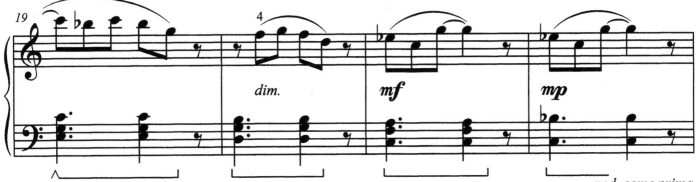

ped. come prima

Soft Pedal Blues 2 / 2

The Cuckoo is a Funny Bird

on an old English Folk Song

arr. Andrew Harbridge

Easy Swing

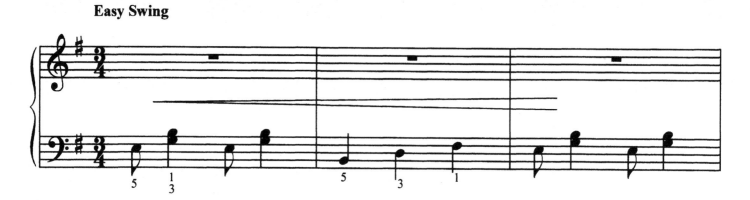

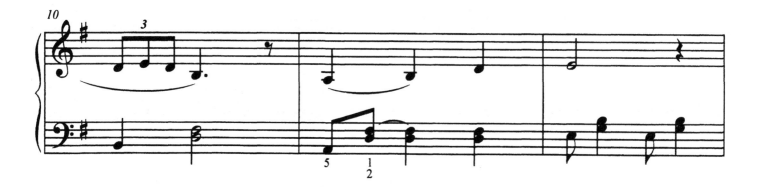

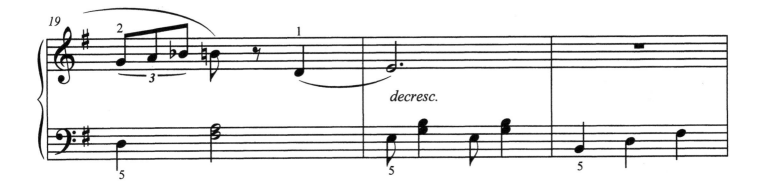

The Cuckoo is a Funny Bird 2 / 2

The Forest at Twilight

Andrew Harbridge

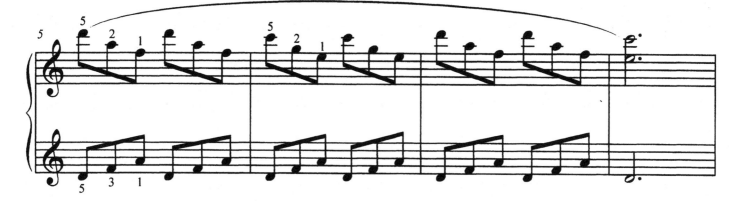

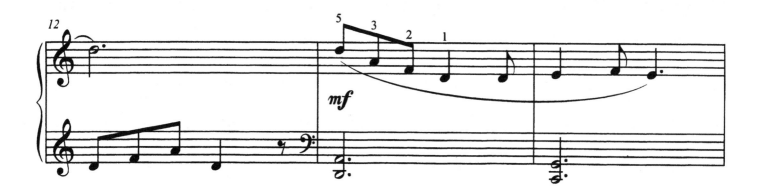

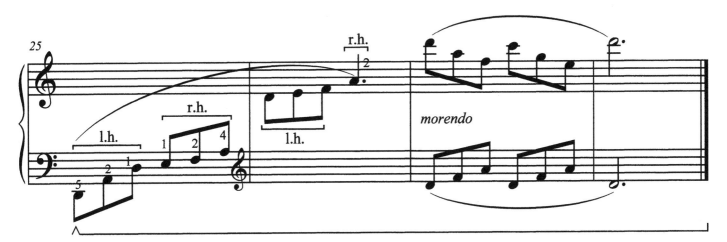

The Forest at Twilight 2 / 2

The Gypsy Daisy

Canadian Folk Song
arr. Fowke/Johnston

The Kelligrews Soiree

Canadian Folk Song
arr. Fowke/Johnston

The Last Waltz

Tyler Seidenberg

Andante cantabile

con pedale

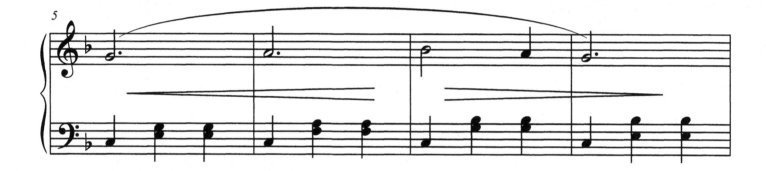

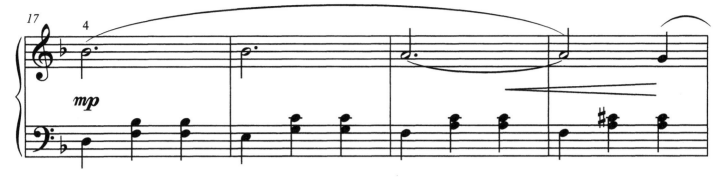

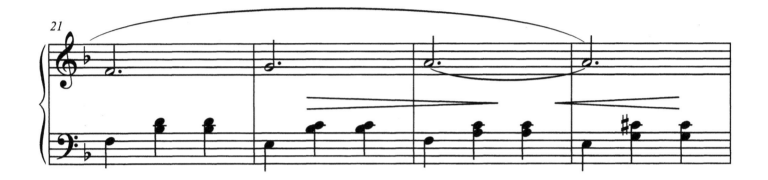

The Last Waltz 2 / 2

Wakeful Cop

Fishel Pustilnik

Moderately, with a blues feel

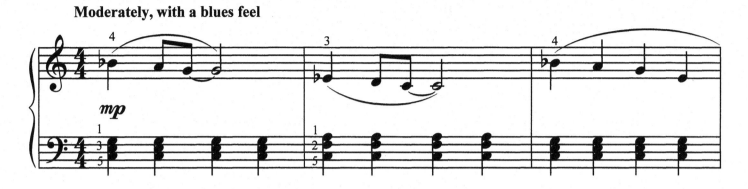

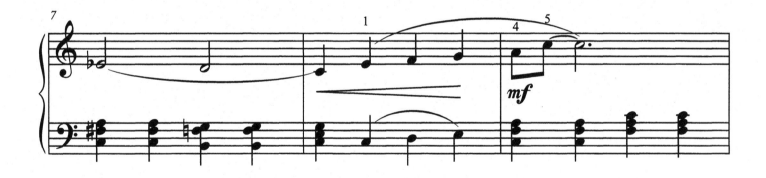

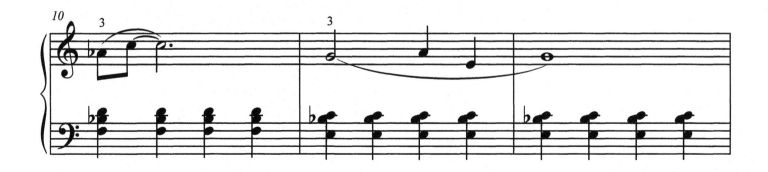

Wakeful Cop 2 / 2

Tuesday Tango

Janet Gieck

Glossary

Ballad – is a slow jazz work characterized by a lyrical melody.

Blues – is a jazz style generally for solo voice. It was often sad and slow, usually utilizing the blues scale or notes and a twelve bar harmonic structure.

Blues Scale – is a predominantly major scale with a flattened third, fifth and seventh notes.

Boogie-Woogie – is a jazz style for the piano with a repeated left hand pattern. Boogie-woogie developed in dance halls during the 1920's and often uses the *twelve bar blues* harmonic structure.

Diatonic Seventh Chords – consist of four notes, a triad with the seventh added above the root. Diatonic seventh chords use only the notes of the scale.

Dixieland – is a type of jazz from around 1912 and is also known as New Orleans or Classic style jazz. It has elements of *ragtime* and *blues*, as well as a distinctive style of *improvisation.*

Improvisation – is a spontaneous production of musical ideas by the performer.

Modes – musical scales developed from early church music, often used and modified by classical and jazz composers. Folk music is often written in modal keys.

Ostinato – is a repeated harmonic, rhythmic or melodic pattern.

Pentatonic Scale – is a scale of five notes, often representing the intervals of the five black keys on the piano. Pentatonic scales are frequently heard in folk music and non-western music.

Ragtime – is one of the earliest forms of jazz, characterized by *syncopated* melodies, *stride bass* and traditional harmonies.

Rock – is a popular style of dance music that developed during the 1950's and is usually based on even eighth note subdivisions. Rock is the simplest derivation of Latin rhythms.

Shuffle Bass – a jazz accompaniment which moves or shuffles back and forth between the same notes.

Stride Bass – is an accompaniment pattern usually found in *ragtime*. It describes the striding motion of the player's left hand.

Swing Rhythm – is a rhythmic technique which grew out the big band era and dance music of the 1930's and 1940's. Rhythm is swung when the beat note is stretched to create a 'long-short' combination. Example: ♫ ♩♪

Syncopation – is the alteration of the natural accent by emphasizing and normally weak beat.

Twelve-Bar Blues – in its simplest form, is a harmonic pattern organized into three four bar phrases. The harmonic pattern is as follows: I - I - I - I   IV - IV - I - I   V - IV - I - I
Colour tones, altered and seventh chords are often included within the pattern.

Walking Bass - a bass line that fills in gaps between successive harmony notes.

SIGN	TERM	DEFINITION
	accent	Emphasize the marked note
	allegretto	Light and lively
	andante	Rather slow, a walking pace
	breathe mark	Break or breathe
	a tempo	Return to the original speed or tempo
	cantabile	Singing style
	con	With
	crescendo/cresc.	Gradually become louder
	diminuendo/dim.	Gradually become softer
	e	And
	espressivo	Expressively
	1st and 2nd ending	Play the first ending and repeat. Then skip the first ending and play the second ending instead
	fermata	Pause on the note or rest
f	forte	Loud
ff	fortissimo	Very loud
	glissando	Drag the finger across the keys
	grace note	Play the small note as quickly as possible, immediately followed by the large note.
l.h.	left hand	Play with the left hand
r.h.	right hand	Play with the right hand
	legato	Smoothly
mf	mezzo forte	Medium loud
mp	mezzo piano	Medium soft
	moderato	Moderate tempo
	morendo	Dying away in time and tone
	moto	Motion
	non	Not
8va	ottava	Play one octave higher than written
8vb		Play one octave lower than written
‖: :‖	repeat signs	Repeat the section within the repeat sign
	Pedale / ped.	Depress the damper or right hand pedal
pp	pianissimo	Very soft
p	piano	Soft
	piu	More
	poco a poco	Little by little
rit.	ritard. / ritardando	Gradually becoming slower
	senza	Without
	staccato	Play the notes short and detached
	subito	Suddenly
	tenuto	Sustained
	triplet	Three notes played in the value of two
	una corda	Soft or left hand pedal